In Level 0, **Step 5** builds previous steps and intro their letters:

j   v   w   x

Special features:

Phonically decodable text builds reading confidence

Short sentences with simple language

Vick has to visit Zelda. Zelda has a bad leg.

Liz and Vick get Zelda into a pen.

We did it!

Repetition of sounds in different words

23

Story Words

Can you match these words to the pictures?

Vick
Liz
The Canyon
Zelda
Nutmeg
bucket
liquid
wet

30

Tricky Words

These tricky words are in the story you have just read. They cannot be phonetically sounded out. Can you memorize them and read them super fast?

the   to
into   we
she   be
             he

31

Summary page to reinforce learning

Practice of words that cannot be sounded out

Phonics and Book Banding Consultant: Kate Ruttle

LADYBIRD BOOKS

UK | USA | Canada | Ireland | Australia
India | New Zealand | South Africa

Ladybird Books is part of the Penguin Random House group of companies
whose addresses can be found at global.penguinrandomhouse.com.

www.penguin.co.uk www.puffin.co.uk www.ladybird.co.uk

A version of this book was previously published as
Fix It Vets – Ladybird I'm Ready for Phonics Level 5, 2014
This edition published 2018
004

A CIP catalogue record for this book is available from the British Library

ISBN: 978-0-241-31248-3

All correspondence to
Ladybird Books
Penguin Random House Children's
80 Strand, London WC2R ORL

Jazz the Vet

Written by Monica Hughes
Illustrated by Ian Cunliffe

Zac and his dad visit Jazz the vet.

Zac's rabbit has a bad leg.

Jazz picks up the rabbit
and rubs the leg.

Jazz tells Zac he can fix the leg. The rabbit gets a jab into the top of his leg.

Val visits the vet. She has a big red parrot. The parrot yells at Jazz.

Get off me!

Jazz has to be quick.
The parrot will nip him.

A man has a big bag.
He unzips the bag.
It has seven kittens in it!

The kittens get jabs and a tub of pills.

Jazz has to put the kittens back into the bag but he has six kittens, not seven!

A kitten was in a big box. She had a nap!

Story Words

Can you match these words
to the pictures?

Zac

Dad

Jazz

rabbit

parrot

kitten

bag

Tricky Words

These tricky words are in the story you have just read. They cannot be sounded out. Can you memorize them and read them super fast?

the   she

he   to

into   be

me

was

Vick the Vet

Written by Monica Hughes
Illustrated by Ian Cunliffe

Vick is a vet. She gets into a van to visit Liz.

Vick

VICK 1

Liz runs The Canyon.

Vick has to visit Zelda.
Zelda has a bad leg.

Liz and Vick get Zelda into a pen.

We did it!

Vick picks up the leg.
The leg has a cut on it.

Vick tells Liz she will fix
the leg.

Vick dabs the cut and puts
a pad on it.

Liz tells Vick she has
to visit Nutmeg.

He is sick.

Vick gets a big pill.
She has to mix it into
the liquid in a bucket.

Nutmeg sucks up the liquid.
He will be well.

Next, Nutmeg sucks up a lot of liquid and . . .

It is a jet of liquid!

Vick is wet, wet, wet!

Story Words

Can you match these words
to the pictures?

Vick

Liz

The
Canyon

Zelda

Nutmeg

bucket

liquid

wet